A Guide to Electronic Maintenance and Repairs

A Guide to Electronic Maintenance and Repairs

A.M. Yusufu and Yunusa Ali S.

PARTRIDGE
A Penguin Random House Company

To order additional copies of this book, contact
Toll Free 800 101 2657 (Singapore)
Toll Free 1 800 81 7340 (Malaysia)
orders.singapore@partridgepublishing.com

www.partridgepublishing.com/singapore

Contents

Dedication

This book is dedicated to Kaduna Polytechnic, Kaduna and Hussaini Adamu Fedearal Polytechnic Kazaure.

Acknowledgements

The Authors gratefully acknowledge Departments of Electrical and Electronics Engineering of Kaduna Polytechnic and Hussaini Adamu Federal Polytechnic Kazaure for their support and cooperation.

Overview

The book offers a good overview of Electronics maintenance and repairs within the curricular, particularly for Diplomas, Higher National Diplomas (HND) and Engineers, who wish to undertake cleaning, basic maintenance, and minor repairs of Electronics devices. This book covers devices and components related to equipment like test instruments and digital equipment. The reader will quickly learn the systematic procedures for identifying causes of faults and the practical methods of repairing them. The content is according to the National curriculum standard (NBTE and NUC) Though most Engineers may still find extensive repairs beyond their interest and ability, this books can help them in maintenance and will teach them more about Electronics maintenance. The book is comprehensive, which takes care of Electronic components and its practical applications. New trend information about components is included. Readers will find the indexes and illustrations (both photos and diagrams) very useful.

Chapter One
FUNCTION AND VALUES OF RESISTORS

1.1 RESISTOR

This chapter gives the basic and fundamentals about resistors as passive components. Resistors are among the general purpose components used in the electronics functional circuitry. They are two-terminal passive electrical components that implement electrical resistance as a circuit element. They act to reduce current flow, while acting to lower voltage levels within circuits. Resistors such as those found in thermistors, varistors, trimmers, photo resistors and potentiometers may have fixed resistances or variable resistances.

The current through a resistor is directly proportional to the voltage across its terminals as represented by Ohm's law:

$$I = \frac{V}{R} \qquad 1$$

In such a way that; I is the current through the conductor in units of amperes, V is the potential difference measured across the conductor in units of volts, and R is the resistance of the conductor in units of ohms (symbol: Ω).

The resistance of a resistor is the ratio of the voltage applied across its terminals to the intensity of current in the circuit, and this can be assumed to be a constant (independent of the voltage) for ordinary resistors working within their ratings given during manufacture. Different values of resistors are identified by means of color coding normally indicated on their surface.

Resistors provide specific values of current and voltage in a circuit prepared to work in current control field. Different designs are available depending on the manufacturer but ratings differ according to application. The significant work done by resistors is to create specified values of current and voltage in a circuit. Figure 1.1 below displayed assorted resistors. The resistors are on millimeter paper, with 1cm spacing to give some idea of the dimensions. Here, figure 1.1a shows some low-power resistors, with power dissipation below 5 watt. Most are cylindrical in shape with a wire protruding from each end for connection to circuit while figure 1.1b shows some higher-power resistors with power dissipation above 5 watt.

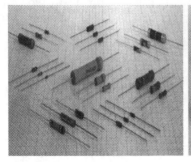 

Figure 1.1: a Some low-power resistors (*Courtesy of microElectronika*) **Figure: 1.1:** b High-power resistors and rheostats (*Courtesy of microElectronika*)

Resistors can either be represented using the American symbol upper or European symbol lower diagram in figure 1.1c below.

Figure 1.1: c Symbols of resistor *(courtesy of microElectronika)*

Based on the data provided in table 1 the value of resistors indicated by color coding can be calculated.

Table: 1: Resistor color coding *(courtesy of microElectronika)*

Color	Value of Each Color	Multiplier	Tolerance Range	Temperature Coefficient (TC)
Silver		x 0.01	±10%	
Gold		x 0.1	±5%	
Black	0	x 1		
Brown	1	x 10	±1%	±100*10-6/K
Red	2	x 100	±2%	±50*10-6/K
Orange	3	x 1 k		±15*10-6/K
Yellow	4	x 10 k		±25*10-6/K
Green	5	x 100 k	±0.5%	
Blue	6	x 1 M	±0.25%	±10*10-6/K
Violet	7	x 10 M	±0.1%	±5*10-6/K
Grey	8	x 100 M		
White	9	x 1 G		±1*10-6/K

Most of available resistors have 4 divisions while some special one has five divisions with first three color indicating digits. The last two divisions are zeros and tolerance respectively. The Surface Mounted Device has limited space usually coated with two or three digits (resistors), at times extra band is added to indicate temperature coefficient. Alternatively, values of resistors can be identified physically in terms of its color coding or by using an Ohmmeter. Since resistor is measured in ohms(Ω), measurements are conducted practically and rated in accordance with standard units of Ohms(Ω), Kilo ohms(KΩ) and Mega Ohms(MΩ).

Decimal points are represented by use of the following letters "R, K and M" while the letter "E" is used to indicate the word "ohm" as shown below.

e.g: 1**R**0 = 1 ohm   4**R**3 = 4.3 ohms   43**R** = 43 ohms
4**k**2 = 4,200 ohms   200**k** = 200,000 ohms
2**M**2 = 2,200,000 ohm

Common resistors have 4 bands. These are shown in figure 1.2 below. First two bands indicate the first two digits of the resistor the third band is the multiplier (number of zeros that are to be added to the number derived from first two bands) and fourth represents the tolerance.

Marking the resistance with five bands is used for resistors with tolerance of 2%, 1% and other high-accuracy resistors. First three bands determine the first three digits, while fourth digit is a multiplier and the fifth digit represents the tolerance.

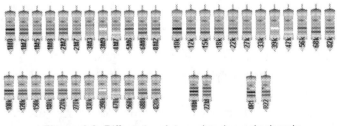

Figure 1.2: Different resistors showing color bands
(*courtesy of microElectronika*)

There are flat surface mounted device(SMD) resistors that have their values written in the outer cover with three digits number having first two numbers as resistor values and the last number as number of zeros present like 174 equivalents to 170000 ohms (170KΩ).

Different kinds of resistors such as E12 and E24 series are normally produced in large quantities. For instance, resistance value of 21 means 0.21, 2.1, 21, 210, 2.1k, 21k, 210k can be represented by 0R21, 2R1, 21R, 21OR, 2K1 and 21K.

Other parameter of resistor specification is its value tolerance which depends on the circuit and can be assigned with 5% 10% etc unless a degree of accuracy is required for specific value of tolerance from the manufacturer.

1.2 POWER DISSIPATION OF RESISTOR

When there is an increase in the current passing through a resistor it gets heated, this may damage or suppress the component if particular value of temperature is reached. Normally, the rating of a resistor in watt is the power dissipated for extended period of time when it is subjected to current control field.

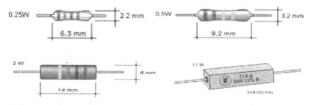

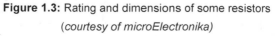

Figure 1.3: Rating and dimensions of some resistors
(*courtesy of microElectronika*)

Some of the ratings in watts of frequently used carbon or wire wound resistors in electronics are 0.125W, 0.25W, 0.5W, 1W, 2W etc. Resistors may have same value but high rating hence these are referred to as the constant or linear resistors. The formulae for power are; P(watt)

$$P = VI \qquad eqn...2$$

$$P = I^2 R \qquad eqn...3$$

$$P = V^2/R \qquad eqn...4$$

Where: V = voltage is measured in volt, I=current in amps and R=resistance in ohms.

Example1; Calculate the power in watt for 10Ω resistor having current of 2A.

$$P= 10X2\text{\textasciicircum}2 =40W \qquad eqn...5$$

1.3 NONLINEAR RESISTORS

The resistors that are designed to change value with a change in temperature or light in circuits are called non linear resistors. This function may not be linear, because there is a change if the voltage or current-flow alters while in operation.

Some non linear resistors include;

1. Negative temperature coefficient resistors (NTC)– This type reduce with increase in temperature.

2. Positive temperature coefficient (PTC)-Increase in temperature leads to increase in resistance.
3. Light dependent resistor (LDR)-Their resistance rise with increase in intensity of light.
4. Voltage dependent resistor (VDR) - This reduces its resistance when it reached a certain limits.

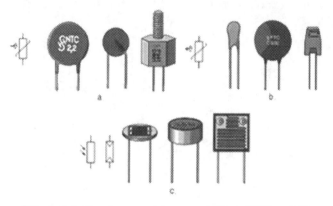

Figure 1.4: Non-linear resistors - a. NTC, b. PTC, c. LDR
(*courtesy of microElectronika*)

Nonlinear resistors can be replaced in a form similar to a transistor containing potentiometer (trimmer), for example a positive temperature coefficient represented by an automobile light and light voltage dependent resistor for open transistor.

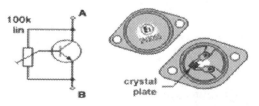

Figure 1.5: Practical applications of resistors
(*courtesy of microElectronika*)

Considering figure 1.6 below which shows a voltage (RC) amplifier designed to amplify low frequency system signal, the system is attached at node 1 and ground with the output on node two. There is a need for calibration of operating point of the transistor for high performance, making voltage in node C that links with ground 0.5 of power supply while adjustment can be made through resistor R1 in the circuit.

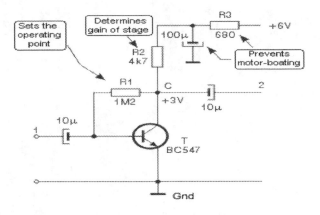

Figure 1.6: Resistor Capacitor amplifier circuit
(*courtesy of microElectronika*)

Amplification level is determined by the resistance R2. The resistor R3 and capacitor (100µF) serve as filtering component to avoid feedback termed as motor- boating and noise is form when it involves more stage.

System instability can result to noise at the output without signal pass to the input due to current flow in the circuit. A tiny waveform is in contact with power rails and move to transistor inputs, hence noise is created. The noise is reduced when more capacitor and resistor combine to each stage in the circuit.

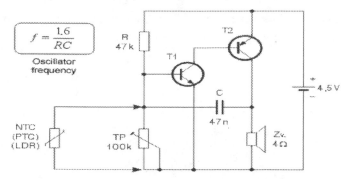

Figure 1.7: Circuit of Alarm that indicated changes in temperature or light (*courtesy of microElectronika*)

Alarm device can be designed when NTC and trimmer potentiometers are attached to the audio oscillator.

Frequency(f)= 1.6/RC=1.6/(47X10^3x47x10^-9)=724HZ

When R=47k and C=47nF,

An increase in oscillator frequency occurs when negative temperature coefficient and potentiometer (trim) are attached to the circuit, Oscillator stops when the trim is at minimum resistance value. For intended temperature, the resistor in the trim should be adjusted for oscillator to begin to work. The circuit negative temperature coefficient (NTC) temperature reduces with increase in resistance and at higher temperature the oscillator is frozen. In doing this, caution should be taken to seal the copper wire from water and other dirty materials.

The positive temperature coefficient can replace NTC, which might apply in refrigerator when particular temperature is set and for any value above this the oscillator will indicate. But light dependent resistor can also be employed for light.

The resistor can be sensitive if there is light when attached to resistance (R). These applications above were resulted from resistance changes due to temperature or presence of light.

1.4 VARIABLE RESISTORS OR POTENTIOMETERS

When connected to electronic circuits, variable resistors also called potentiometers are used to adjust current or voltage.

These are some categories of available potentiometers

1. Coated potentiometer; The resistive material is embedded in insulator body with a slider moving from one end of resistive material to the other which leads to increase or decrease in resistance. It is widely use in audio amplifier and radio transistor receiver mostly contains linear resistance or logarithmic that is determined by the position of slider.
2. Wire-wound potentiometer; it is similar with coated potentiometer but it is a conductor wire place around the insulator. This is used where accuracy is more needed when control and have large dissipation values.

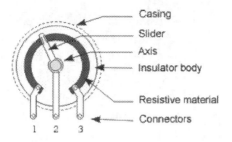

Figure: 1.8: Coated potentiometer (*courtesy of microElectronika*)

The potentiometer resistance are E6 types in addition to 1, 2.2,1 4.7 having tolerance value ranging from 30% to 10% for coated type and 5% for wire wound type.

Figure: 1.9: The Potentiometers (*courtesy of microElectronika*)

In figure 1.8 represents a model of two pots in one casing stereo potentiometers. They have sliders mounted on shared axis that would enable them to move and regulate the right and left channels simultaneously. However, they can be used in stereophonic amplifiers. The lower left is the called slider potentiometer while the one at the lower right is a wire-wound pot with a power of 20Watts commonly used as rheostat (for regulating current while charging a battery etc). There are small potentiometers

23

with a slider that is adjusted via a screwdriver. They are used in circuits that demand very accurate voltage and current values, also trimmer potentiometers (or just *trim pots*) are used. Trim pots also come in many different shapes and sizes, with wattage ranging from 0.1W to 0.5W. Several different trim pots, along with the symbols are shown in figure 1.10 below.

Figure 1.10: Trim potentiometers *(courtesy of. microElectronika)*

Apart from trim pot that use plastic shaft for fine tuning, the resistance of these trimmers can be altered by the use of precision screwdriver.

1.5 APPLICATION OF POTENTIOMETERS

Some applications of potentiometer are for tuning, change in volume and so on. As illustrated in figure 1.12 below the potentiometer labeled *bass* adjusts low frequency amplification, if the slider is placed at lowest position, the mid frequency signals is 1/10 of tiny low frequency signals. Whenever the slider is placed at highest value, the mid frequency signal is in tenth fold of tiny low frequency amplification. For potentiometer labeled *treble* it adjusts high frequency amplification. The graph describes relationship between low, mid and high frequency amplification signal input to the system.

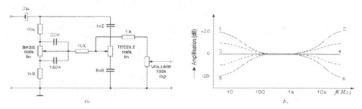

Figure 1.11: Schematic circuit & graph for regulating tone
(*courtesy of microElectronika*)

Potentiometers are used for tuning, change in volume etc. It is illustrated in the diagram below The potentiometer labeled *bass* adjusts low frequency amplification, if the slider is placed at lowest position, the mid frequency signals is 1/10 of tiny low frequency signals. When the slider is placed at highest value, the mid frequency signal is in tenfold of tiny low frequency amplification of the circuit.

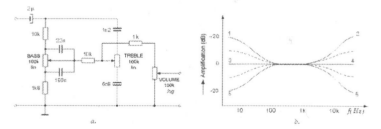

Figure 1.12: Circuit for regulating tone (*courtesy of microElectronika*)

Adjustment of high frequency amplification is done using potentiometer labeled *treble*. The graph describes relationship between low, mid and high frequency amplification signal.

Chapter Two

RATING AND APPLICATIONS
OF A CAPACITOR

2.1 CAPACITORS

The function of capacitors is to store electric charge as voltage. They posses capacitance and are widely used in electrical electronics application. The reactance of capacitor Xc is inversely proportion to the frequency as shown:

$$X_C = \frac{1}{2\pi f C} \qquad \text{eqn...6}$$

F= frequency in (Hertz), C= capacitance in (Farad).

For instance, a capacitor has reactance of 5nF at f =125-kHz will be;

$$X_C = \frac{1}{2 \cdot 3.14 \cdot 125000 \cdot 5 \cdot 10^{-9}} = 255\,\Omega,$$

while, at f=1.25MHz, it equals

$$X_C = \frac{1}{2 \cdot 3.14 \cdot 1250000 \cdot 5 \cdot 10^{-9}} = 25.5\,\Omega.$$

Capacitor as a passive component is used for filtering, amplifying, oscillating, rectification in circuit etc and it has infinite value of reactance for direct current. The smaller values of capacitors have their unit in *micro, nano and pico* farads as shown below:

For instance; 1μF=10^-6, 1nF=10^-9F and 1pF=10^-12F.

Alternatively represented as 3n2 =3.2nFn35 =0.35Nf or 0.6u=o.6Mf.

Other simpler notation system is used as with resistors. If the mark on the capacitor is 120 the value is 120pF, 1n2 stands for 1.2nF, n22 stands for 0.22nF, while .1μ (or .1u) stands for 0.1μF.

2.2 SIMPLE BLOCK-CAPACITORS

Capacitors that have constant value are formed with parallel plate separated by an insulator of different materials which is the base for naming a capacitor.

Figure 2.1: Fixed capacitors (*courtesy of microElectronika*)

2.3 SOME VALUES OF BLOCK-CAPACITORS

The values of capacitors are indicated by digits with their maximum working voltage and additional parameters like temperature coefficient, tolerance etc while smallest one has no marking but kept in their packet until the need arise. The capacitor values are independent of their sizes and vary from one manufacturer to the other based on the materials they are made from.

Although some manufacturers might not specify the working voltage due to low direct current or voltage supply system for a particular capacitor. There are capacitors with four division values coding and five values coding system, for tubular type with five bands, the first color give the tolerance as shown in figure 2.2 and table 2.1 below.

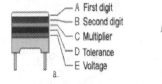 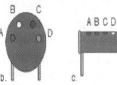

Figure 2.2: Color-coded value of capacitors

(*courtesy of microElectronika*)

Table: 2.1: Four and Five division values coding of Capacitors
(*courtesy of microElectronika*)

COLOR	DIGIT	MULTIPLIER	TOLERANCE(%	VOLTAGE(V
Black	0	Multiply by 1 pF	± 20	
Brown	1	.10 pF	± 1	
Red	2	.100 pF	± 2	250
Orange	3	.1 nF	± 2.5	
Yellow	4	.10 nF		400
Green	5	.100 nF	± 5	
Blue	6	.1 μF		
Violet	7	.10 μF		
Grey	8	.100 μF		
White	9	.1000 μF	± 10	

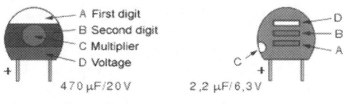

Figure 2.3: Marking the tantalum capacitors

(courtesy of microElectronika)

Table: 2.2: Color-coded values of tantalum capacitors
(courtesy of microElectronika)

COLOR	DIGIT	MULTIPLIER(μF	VOLTAGE(V
Black	0	x 1	10
Brown	1	x 10	
Red	2	x 100	
Orange	3		
Yellow	4		6.3
Green	5		16
Blue	6		20
Violet	7		
Grey	8	x .01	25
White	9	x .1	3
Pink			35

The maximum working voltage must be greater than voltage across the capacitor. Note that the voltage across a capacitor must not exceed the maximal working voltage as the capacitor may get destroyed. When the voltage is not known, the least case should be taken into account. Sometimes due to malfunction of some other component in circuit, it happens that the voltage on capacitor equals the power supply voltage. For instance let the supply voltage be 16V, this means that 16V is the maximum working voltage for that particular capacitor.

2.4 ELECTROLYTIC CAPACITORS

These types of capacitors have fixed value with positive and negative poles, the positive poles must be connected to higher voltage side compare to negative pole and the reverse connection will cause the insulating layer inside the capacitor to dissolve and the capacitor will be permanently damaged. Although they have other uses in circuits but they are predominantly used in filtering.

Electrolytic capacitors can have exceptionally high capacity, ranging from one to several thousand µF. Because they are polarized components, meaning they have positive and negative leads, which is very important when connecting it to a circuit as outlined above. This shows that connecting it to a voltage source that exceeds its working voltage explosion may also occur. In order to prevent such instances, one of the capacitor's connectors is very clearly marked with a (+) or (−), while the working voltage is printed on their cases. In figure 2.4 below, some models of electrolytic capacitors, as well as their symbols are shown.

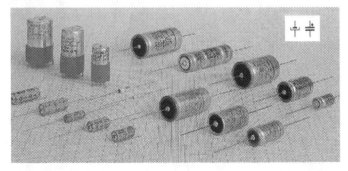

Figure 2.4: Electrolytic capacitors (*courtesy of microElectronika*)

2.5 VARIABLE CAPACITORS

These types have capacity values from 10^{-12} to 5×10^{-10} with different shapes and sizes. They contain stator and movable plates that are fitted for easy decouple from mesh when the shaft is rotating ie varying the capacitance value. Their dielectric is usually air or plastic thin layer.

They are capacitors with variable capacity. Their minimal capacity ranges from 1p and their maximum capacity goes as high as few hundred pF (500pF). These types of capacitors usually come in various shapes and sizes from the manufacturer. When adjusting these capacitors, it is important that the plates do not touch.

Below are photos of air-dielectric capacitors as well as mylar-insulated variable capacitors (2.5a).

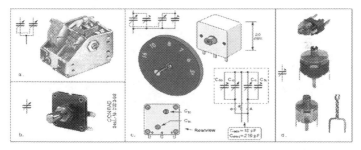

Figure 2.5: Variable capacitors with Trimmer knobs
(*courtesy of microElectronika*)

One of the capacitor types is called (ganged capacitor) possessing two capacitors rotating simultaneously. This capacitor is used normally in radio receivers while the larger ones are used for tuning. Mini types of capacitors are also available for uses in oscillator circuits.

Series of variable capacitors have solid insulator instead of air dielectric fixed between movable plates and stator that are resistance to fault caused by mechanical means.

In radio receivers, frequency is regulated by variable capacitor. Semi-variable capacitors although tiny have values that are up to 10Pico-farads which found application in tuning radio receiver and transmitters.

2.6 CAPACITOR PRACTICAL ILLUSRATION

Consider 5µF electrolytic capacitor in figure that provides flow of signal from one stage to the other and disallows the passage of direct current from one stage to the other. It acts like resistances of very low and high values for both signal and direct current respectively.

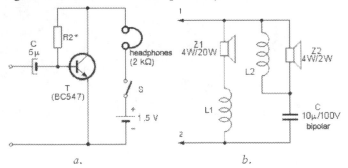

Figure 2.6: a Amplifier with headphones, b Electrical band-switch
(*courtesy of microElectronika*)

In figure 2.6b, Z_1 and Z_2 are speakers while L_1, L_2 and C (capacitor) pave way for low and mid-frequency for speaker Z_1 with high frequency signal pass to Z_2. The terminal 1 and 2 are joined to amplifier output (audio). The high frequency current corresponds to high impedance with low reactance of the capacitors, in this case current pass to Z_2. The reverse case occurs for low frequency signal, current will pass through Z_1 for this instance.

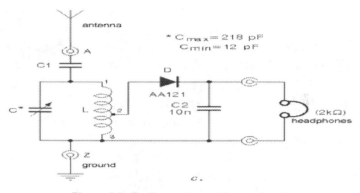

Figure 2.7: Radio-receiver detector circuits
(courtesy of microElectronika)

Figure 2.9 above is termed as crystal set with coil L and variable capacitor (C) serving as oscillatory circuit for tuning the frequency. Different station could be reached by using the rotor in the capacitor.

Chapter Three
THE COILS AND TRANSFORMERS

3.1 COILS

The predominant areas of use for coils and transformers include transmitter, oscillator, and radio receivers and so on.

Coils are wound round a former with numbers of turns of copper wire having inductance that can be measured in micro-Henry (μH), mili-Henry and Henry.

Inductance of coil can be determined by;

$$X_L = 2\pi fL \qquad\qquad eqn\ldots 7$$

Where f=frequency with L as an inductance

The numbers of turn in single layer coil with hole inserted where ends are placed to avert unwinding is shown in figure 3.1a below while figure 3.1b depicted a picture of joint end of one coil to the initial point of the other coil.

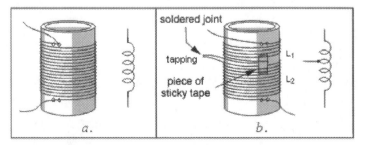

Figure 3.1: Single-layer coils (*courtesy of microElectronika*)

Figure 3.2 contains a multilayered coil with an opening where ferromagnetic core can be placed to give rise to inductance when the core is adjusted. The high frequency transformer consists of two coils that are magnetically linked together, each having separate ferromagnetic core which can be altered.

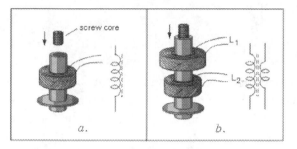

Figure 3.2: Multi-layered coil containing core and coupled coils (*courtesy of microElectronika*)

Coils of thickness around 0.55mm and inductance can be varying using squeezing or stretching while coil of frequency greater than 50MHertz and inductance will be small with few turns.

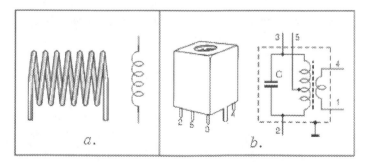

Figure 3.3: High frequency coil and Inter-frequency transformer (*courtesy of microElectronika*)

Two coils in metal casing are shown in figure 3.3 above. An oscillatory circuit is realized by the parallel combination of capacitor (C) and the coil facing it while the other coil allow signal flow to next stage. Instead of connecting the undesired signal flow to earth, the metal structure avoids it. It found application in radio receiver and similar equipment.

A ferrite is a pot core inductor with kind of ferromagnetic core shown in figure 3.4 below. The inductor has two separate halves coil combine together and is designed to withstand frequency to maximum limits of 100 kilo-Hertz. In order to vary inductance the top screw can be adjusted.

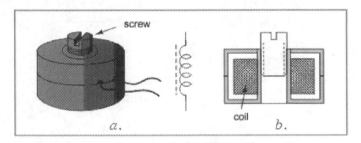

Figure 3.4: A "pot core" inductor (*courtesy of microElectronika*)

3.2 SIMPLE TRANSFORMERS

An electrical device that transfers energy between two circuits is called a transformer. This energy transfer is done through electromagnetic induction. A transformer can transform electric power from one circuit to the other with same frequency. It is a stationary piece of component that consists of two windings of wire which are wound around a common core to provide tight electromagnetic coupling between the windings. This core material is often a laminated iron core. The coil that receives the electrical input energy is referred to as the primary winding, while the output coil is called the secondary winding. The larger voltage higher number of turns is the primary side while secondary side has low voltage and less number of turns for use in electronic circuitry.

Figure 3.5: Transformers in various sizes
(*courtesy of microElectronika*)

A transformer is a safe and efficient voltage converter mostly consisting of iron core ferromagnetic materials, and may be used to change the AC voltage at its input to a higher or lower voltage at its output.

Figure 3.6 below shows number of secondary voltages which may occur in a given transformer.

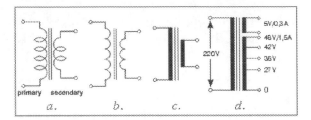

Figure 3.6: Symbols of a transformer (*courtesy of microElectronika*)

3.2.1 Characteristics and principles of a transformer

Two coils at primary and secondary side of a transformer are magnetically linked together. The primary is an alternating voltage source and when one of the coils is connected to it, an alternating flux is set up which linked with the other coil to produce mutual induced electromotive force (*e.m.f*). Current will flow that is electrically transferred to the terminal of other coil.

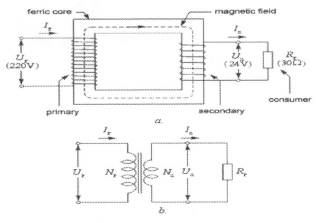

Figure 3.7: Circuit of a transformer and its symbol
(*courtesy of microElectronika*)

An iron core that has lower magnetic resistance when compared to air is used to transfer to the secondary all the magnetic field form from primary side so as to avoid heat losses. In most cases, high voltage equipment utilized high voltage values while for electronic components lesser voltage is required at the secondary. The relationships between voltage, number of turns and current are;

$$V_2/V_1 = N_2/N_1 = I_1/I_2 = K \qquad \text{eqn...8}$$

In such a way that V_2, N_2, I_2 represent voltage, number of turns and current in the secondary side with V_1, N_1, I_1 for voltage, number of turns and current in the primary side respectively.

Their power rating can be deducted from;

$$P = V_2 X I_2 = V_1 X I_1 \qquad \text{eqn...9}$$

The ratio of the two power provide their efficiency which cannot be 100% due to fatalities like eddy current loss.

Efficiency= power in the secondary coil/ power in the primary side

Maximum current of the transformer can be found by dividing the power rating by secondary voltage practically.

3.3 COILS AND TRANSFORMERS PRACTICAL EXAMPLES

Following our last discussion it was realized that coils and capacitor serve as filters which allow passage of currents in the speakers. However oscillator circuit is generated from parallel combination of the coil with capacitor (C), and then amplifies certain radio signal as in figure 3.8 below.

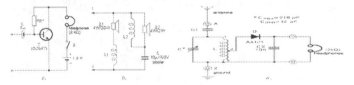

Figure 3.8: Amplifier contains headphones, the Band-switch and the Detector radio-receiver *(courtesy of microElectronika)*

Practical application of transformer in rectifying circuit as depicted in figure 3.9 below.

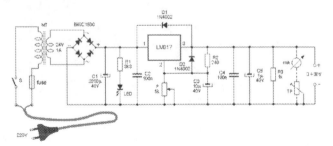

Figure 3.9: Stabilized converter involving circuit LM317 *(courtesy of microElectronika)*

Linear potentiometer may be varying using the output direct current (P) say 3-30v

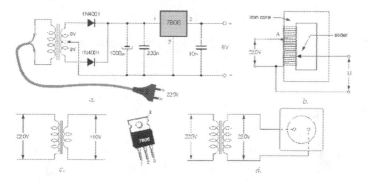

Figure 3.10: Stabilize converters having regulator 7806, the auto-transformer, and transformer with secondary voltage of 110v and isolating transformer (*courtesy of microElectronika*)

The above figure shows a center- type rectification in the secondary coil by the use of 2 diodes. The second one represent auto transformer, having common winding for both primary and secondary parts. It involves less copper and the voltage can be varied through slider with slider at starting point equivalent to zero voltage, but increments occur as the slider move up. The last one totally isolated from main supply is unity as the output is the same with input.

41

Chapter Four
TYPES OF TRANSISTORS AND THEIR APPLICATION

4.1 TRANSISTOR

Transistors are widely used in many applications such as switches, modulating signal, oscillating system etc. They are semiconductor device with two poles (bipolar). Semiconductor devices are made from silicon or germanium as a result of doping and sandwich activities of the P-N junction.

Transistors are of two types;

1. PNP transistors
2. NPN transistor

Figure 4.1: various transistors devices (*courtesy of microElectronika*)

Bipolar transistor consists of collector C, emitter E and base B. At times some transistors are earthed. Nowadays component description and specification are checked online and replacement or equivalent for substitute can be easily done.

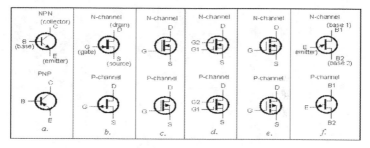

Figure 4.2: Transistor symbols consist of bipolar, FET, - MOSFET, dual gate MOSFET, inductive channel MOSFET and single connection transistor (*courtesy of microElectronika*)

Consider figure 4.1 above, when coding transistor the 2nd letter indicates its main purpose as in c. for low and medium power LF transistor, D for high power LF transistor, f. for low power HF transistor D for other transistors, L for high power HF transistors, P for photo transistor, S for switch transistor, U for high voltage transistor. Other coding; AC540 for germanium core, LF, low power, BC107 for silicon, LF, low power 3/10W, BSY54 for silicon switching transistor etc. In summary, different part of the world have their separate coding arrangement.

A.M. YUSUFU AND YUNUSA ALI S.

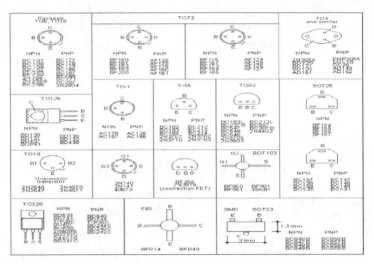

Figure 4.3: Common transistors packages
(*courtesy of microElectronika*)

The TO-3 package contain 2 pins each for base and emitter and used as covering for high power transistor while the collector is attached to package, and then screwed to the circuit through one bond to the heat-sink. Surface mount devices have brought great improvement of using mini-component in place of bigger size which is cost effective. Using special soldering avoid the set back of these kinds of component. Another important provision is that NPN transistor can be replaced with NPN having same polar arrangement.

4.2 WORKING PRINCIPLE OF A TRANSISTOR

In an analog system, transistor serves as regulator in power supply and as switches in various circuits. An experimental set up in figure 4.4 below contains potentiometer, resistor and light bulb used to illustrate the operation of transistor.

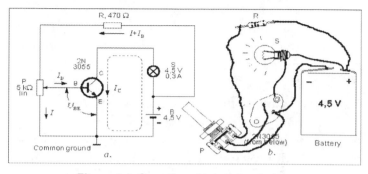

Figure 4.4: Operation of transistor devices
(courtesy of microElectronika)

In order to avoid over voltage that will spoil the transistor, Resistor (R) is offered to the circuit due to silicon working with maximum voltage of 0.6V base-emitter voltage (V_{be}).

In support of initial position of potentiometer, the V_{be} is zero (current = 0), as the position rises V_{be} steadily increase to 0.6V and the light will be coming up. When the knob increases, the bulb becomes brighter with V_{be} getting to 0.75V.

From the experiment, the following parameters can be obtained: V_{be}, collector-emitter voltage V_{ce}, collector current I_c base current I_b and other transistor characteristics can be deduced.

The next experiment number two consists of 1 x 10^6 ohm resistor, BC107, electrolytic capacitor (ten to hundred micro farad) and power source for low frequency amplifying circuit as depicted in figure 4.5 below. The operation is similar with first experiment, but headphone is connected to collector terminal and 1M resistor is placed between base and collector having 0.6/4µA at the base. The sum of current in the base and collector gives emitter current with gain of 250. Due to lesser current flow in base, and then $I_c=I_e$, also $I_c/I_b=H_{fe}$. But $I_c=1_{mA}$.

H_{fe}= current amplification coefficient of transistor.

As the headphone is switch on, the voltage will be felt at terminal 1 with 50Hertz frequency (AC source) and then amplify by the transistor. As for the base of transistor 2 separate voltages is going in, one from resistor 1M and the other one from terminal 1. Due to this collector current can be varied to lower or higher value 50 times per seconds. Thus low frequency tone could be obtained from terminal 1 and 2.

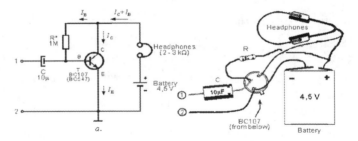

Figure 4.5: Transistor as an amplifier (*courtesy of microElectronika*)

4.3 CHARACTERISTICS OF TRANSISTORS

In trying to work with transistors, the following criteria should be taken into consideration:

1) Maximum power rating 2) current amplification 3) maximum voltage of (V_{ce}) and 4) collector current, the essence is to make circuit that will not exceed maximum values of transistor characteristics. So V_{ce} x I_c should be lower than maximum power value of transistor. The heat sink in transistor is applicable for cooling the heat generated by transistor for which reduction in current or voltage cannot meet up.

By using multimeter current amplification coefficient can be determined in the circuit below so that it will measure direct current to level of 5mA. The two diodes (IN4001) combine with 1000Ω resistor protect the set up. If the switch is closed, current pass to the base. There is need to reverse the polarity of the battery and probe for PNP transistor when using analog (multimeter), but negative sign indicates digital change in polarity.

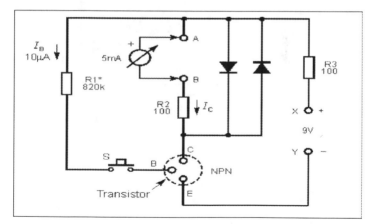

Figure 4.6: Evaluating H_{fe} (*courtesy of microElectronika*)

4.4 TRANSISTORS TESTING USING AN EFFICIENT TECHNIQUE

As illustrated in figure 4.7 below, a transistor is connected to the circuit. T2 represents transistor to be tested and the light emitting diode will glow for connecting good transistor to circuit. For PNP transistor, the light emitting diode, the two capacitors and their polarity should be changed and transistor T1 should be replace with proper polarity.

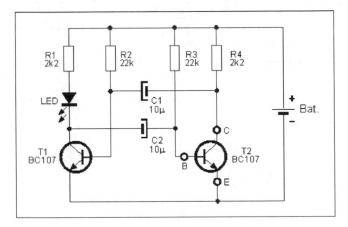

Figure 4.7: Technique of testing transistors (*courtesy of microElectronika*)

4.5 TUN and TUP

Some terminologies used by many author for indicating general usage of transistor as in Transistor Universal for NPN (TUN) while Transistor Universal for PNP represented by TUP are briefly explained. Their characteristics are maximum power is 100Mw, maximum voltage between collector and emitter equal 20V, minimum gain 110, maximum collector current 100Ma and minimum frequency of 100MHertz.

Examples of tune are BC107[8,9], BC382 [3,4], BC317[8,9], BC207[8,9], BC182[3,4], 2N3860, 2N3947 and so on.

For TUP we have; BC212[3,4], BC512[3,4], BC320 [1,2], BC350[1,2], 2N2412, 2N3906 etc.

4.6 APPLICATION OF TRANSISTOR IN PRACTICE

Figure 4.8 below describes a significant feature known as amplification while employing transistor on analog devices.

There is an oscillating circuit created from capacitor and the coil meant for tuning the radio station. A detector is created from diode, capacitor (100PF) and resistor (470k) for low frequency signal. There is clear difference between common ground and the grounding, the common ground is attached to the circuit board via copper strip (wider track) while the ground consists of metallic rod put inside a wet earth. R_2 biases the transistor in this arrangement.

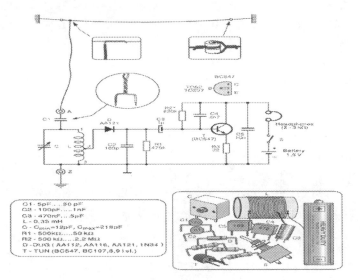

Figure 4.8: Transistor amplifying circuit and Detector

(*courtesy of microElectronika*)

Chapter Five
SEMICONDUTOR DIODE TYPES AND APPLICATION

5.1 DIODES

Diode is another important semiconductor device like transistors. They are fabricated from semi-conducting material. So, the first letter in their recognition is "A" for germanium diode or "B" for silicon diode. They can be cashed in glass, metal or a plastic housing. They have two leads: cathode (k) and an anode (A). The most important property of all diodes is their resistance is very low in one direction and very large in the opposite direction. For instance, if a diode is measured with a multimeter and it reads a low value of ohms, this is not really the resistance of the diode but represents the voltage drop across the junction of the diode. This means if the junction is not damaged a multimeter can be used to detect it. A diode is operational if the reading is low in one direction and very high in the other direction.

If a diode is placed in a circuit and the voltage on the anode is higher than the cathode, it acts like a low value resistor and current will flow.

Current does not flow if it is connected in the opposite direction. In this manner it acts like a large value resistor.

For the first case the diode is said to be "forward biased" and in the second case it is "reverse biased." So when a diode is forward biased it conducts, but when it is reverse biased it does not conduct. Several different diodes are shown in Figure 5.1 below:

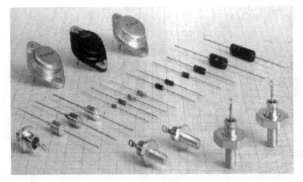

Figure 5.1: Types of diodes (*courtesy of microElectronika*)

Single diodes are depicted above; however 4 diodes are available in a single package. This is called a BRIDGE or BRIDGE RECTIFIER. Examples of a bridge are shown in the diagram below:

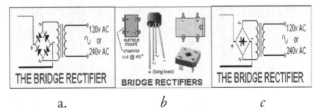

a.   *b*   *c*

Figure 5.2: Bridge rectifiers casing (*courtesy of microElectronika*)

When inserting it into a circuit one must be able to identify each of the 4 leads on a bridge so that it can be around the correct way. The surface-mount device above is identified by a cut @ 45° along one side. The leaded bridge has one leg longer than the others and the top is marked with AC marks and "+." The high-current bridge has a corner cut off and the other surface-mount device has a cut or notch at one end. Figure 5.2b shows how these devices are added to a circuit.

A single diode can be shown on the circuit diagram when 4 diodes face the same direction as shown in figure 5.2c.

Several numbers of specially-designed diodes including those for high current, high-speed, low voltage-drop, light-detection, and varying capacitance as the voltage is altered are available. Because silicon can withstand high temperature, most diodes are made from it however; germanium is used if a low voltage-drop is required. Another different type of diode is a light emitting diode called a LED. Figure 5.3 below depicted the different diode types.

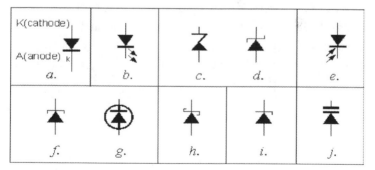

Figure: 5.3: Diode symbols: a - standard diode, b - LED, c, d - Zener, e - photo, f, g - tunnel, h - Schottky, i - breakdown, j – capacitive (*courtesy of microElectronika*)

The construction of Light Emitting Diodes emanated from a crystalline substance that emits light when a current flows through it. Though it depends on the crystalline material the colors red, yellow, green, blue or orange light is produced as shown in the photo in figure 5.4a below.

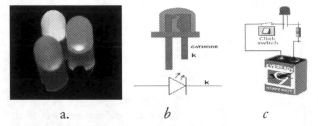

a.   b   c

Figure: 5.4: a. LED different colors b. LED symbols c. LED resistor test
(*courtesy of microElectronika*)

White light cannot be produced from any of these materials, so a triad of red, blue and green is placed inside a case and they are all illuminated at the same time to produce white light. Nowadays, by a very complex and interesting process white light has been produced from LEDs having a cathode and anode lead and these are normally connected to DC around the correct way. The cathode lead is shorter and can be identified on the body by a flat-spot on the side of the LED.

Among the most important things to remember about a LED is the characteristic voltage that appears across it when connected to a voltage. This cannot be altered and does not change with brightness. For a red LED, this voltage is 1.7v and if you supply it with more than this voltage, it will be damaged. The easy solution is to place a resistor on one lead as shown in figure 5.4c above.

In this arrangement the LED will allow the exact voltage to appear across it and the brightness will depend on the value of the resistor chosen.

The Zener diodes of figure 5.3c and d are designed to stabilize a voltage. Diodes marked as ZPD5.6V or ZPY15V have operating voltages of 5.6V and 15V respectively.

The constructions of photo diodes shown in figure 5.3e are in a way that they allow light to fall on the P-N connection. When there is no light, a photo diode acts as a normal diode. It has high resistance in one direction, and low resistance in opposite direction. When there is light, both resistances are low. Photo diodes and LEDs are the main items in an opt coupler (to be discussed in more detail later). Tunnel diodes (5.3f and 5.3g) are generally used in oscillators for very high frequencies. The Schottky diodes of figure 5.3h have low voltage drop in the forward direction and are used in high frequency circuits and for its Breakdown diodes in 5.2i are actually Zener diodes. They pass current only when voltage rises above a pre-defined value and used in various devices for safety and voltage regulation.

Varicap diode in figure 5.3j is used instead of a variable capacitor in high frequency circuits. When the voltage across it is changed, the capacitance between cathode and anode is changed. This diode is frequently used in transceivers oscillators and radio receivers.

The cathode of a low power diode can best be tested it with a multimeter although it is marked with a ring painted on the case, but it is worth noting that some manufacturers label the anode this way, so it is Power diodes are marked with a symbol engraved on the housing. If a diode is housed in a metal package, the case is usually the cathode and anode is the lead coming from the cover.

5.2 How to identify a diode

Diodes from Europe are marked using two or three letters and a number. The first letter is used to make out the material used in manufacturing the component (A - germanium, B - silicon), or, in case of letter Z, a Zener diode. The second and third letters indicate the type and usage of the diode. Varieties of diodes include:

A - Low power diode, like the *AA111*, *AA113*, *AA121*, etc. - they are used in the detector of a radio receiver; *BA124, BA125*: Varicap diodes used instead of variable capacitors in receiving devices, oscillators, etc., *BAY80, BAY93*, etc. - switching diodes used in devices using logic circuits. *BA157, BA158*, etc. - these are switching diodes with short recovery time.

B - Two capacitive (Varicap) diodes in the same housing, like *BB104, BB105*, etc. Y - Regulation diodes, like *BY240, BY243, BY244*, etc. - these regulation diodes come in a plastic packaging and operate on a maximum current of 0.8A. If there is another *Y*, the diode is planned for higher current. For example, *BYY44* is a diode whose absolute maximum current rating is 1A. When *Y* is the second letter in a Zener diode mark (*ZY10, ZY30*, etc.) it means it is intended for higher current. G, G, PD

- different tolerance marks for Zener diodes. Some of these are *ZF12* (5% tolerance), *ZG18* (10% tolerance), *ZPD9.1* (5% tolerance). The third letter is used to indicate a property (high current, for example). The American markings begin with 1N followed by a number, *1N4001*, for example (regulating diode), *1N4449* (switching diode), etc. Japanese style is similar to American however; the main difference is that instead of N there is S, *1S241* as indication.

5.3 Characteristics of a Diode

An essential characteristic when using power diodes is the maximum current in the forward direction (IF_{max}) and maximum voltage in the reverse direction (VR_{max}). While the important characteristics for a Zener diode are Zener voltage (V_Z), Zener current (I_Z) and maximum dissipation power (P_D).

It is necessary to know the maximum and minimum capacitance when working with capacitive diodes, as well as values of DC voltage during which these capacitances take place.

The expected characteristic voltage across a LED depends on the color and starts at 1.7V for red to more than 2.4V for green and blue. It is equally essential to know the maximum value of current the LED is capable of passing. Current starts at 1mA for a very small glow and goes to about 40mA. High brightness LEDs and "power LEDs" require up to 1 amp and more. Knowing the exact current required by the LED to be used is important as the wrong dropper resistor will allow too much current to flow and the LED will be damaged directly. There are universal diodes beside universal transistors TUN and TUP (mentioned in Chapter 4.5). On their circuit diagrams they are marked with DUS (for universal silicon diode) and DUG (for germanium diode). *DUS = Diode Universal Silicon   DUG = Diode Universal Germanium*

5.4 Diodes in practical circuit

The circuit diagram of a power supply in figure (3.9) uses several diodes. The first four are in a single package, recognized by *B40C1500*. This is a bridge rectifier. The LED in the circuit indicates the transformer is working. Resistor R1 is used to limit the current through the LED and the brightness of the LED indicates the approximate voltage. Diodes marked *1N4002* protects the integrated circuit.

Consider figure 5.5 below which shows some other examples of diodes. The life of a globe can be improved by adding a diode as shown in 5.5a. By simply connecting it in series, the current passing through the globe is halved and it lasts a lot longer. Nevertheless the brightness is reduced and the light becomes yellow. The Diode should have a reverse voltage of over 400V and a current higher than the globe so *1N4004* or *BY244* is appropriate. The circuit of 5.5c can represent a very simple DC voltage stabilizer for low currents as a reference.

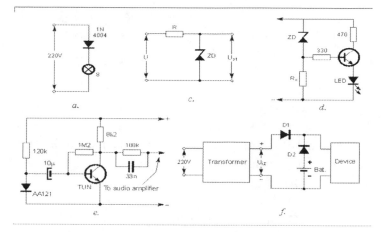

Figure 5.5: a - using a diode to prolong the light bulb's life span, b - stair-light LED indicator, c - voltage stabilizer, d - voltage rise indicator, e - rain noise synthesizer, f - backup supply (*courtesy of microElectronika*)

Note that; un-stabilized voltage is marked "U", and stabilized "U_{st}." Voltage on the Zener diode is equal to U_{st}, so to achieve a stabilized 9V, use a *ZPD9.1* diode. Although this stabilizer has limited use it is the basis of all designs found in power supplies. The other known as voltage overload detector shown in figure 5.5d can also be done. In this case LED indicates when a voltage is over a predefined value. Once the voltage is lower than the operating voltage of the Zener, it acts as a high value resistor, so DC voltage on the base of the transistor is very low, and the transistor does not "turn on." When the voltage rises to equal the Zener voltage, its resistance is lowered, and transistor receives current on its base and it turns on to light up the LED. This example uses a 6V Zener diode, which means that the LED is illuminated when the voltage reaches that value. For other voltage

59

values, different Zener diodes should be used. Brightness and the exact moment of illuminating the LED can be set with the value of resistor Rx.

Modification of this circuit can be done so that it shows signals when a voltage drops below some predefined level, the Zener diode and Rx are swapped. For instance, by using a 12V Zener diode, a car battery level indicator can be made. In this case the battery is ready for recharge when the voltage drops below 12V.

A noise-producing circuit, which produces a rain-like sound, is represented in figure 5.5e. The DC current flowing through diode *AA121* isn't absolutely constant and this creates the noise which is amplified by the transistor (any NPN transistor used) and passed to a filter (resistor-capacitor circuit with values 33nF and 100k). Figure 5.5f shows a battery back-up circuit. Whenever the "supply" fails, the battery takes over the operation.

Chapter Six
Sample of Thyristors, triacs, diacs

Consider figure 6.1a and b below, where several thyristors are displayed. It can be seen that Triacs look the same, while diacs look like small power rectifying diodes. Figure 6.2 shows their symbols, and pin-out.

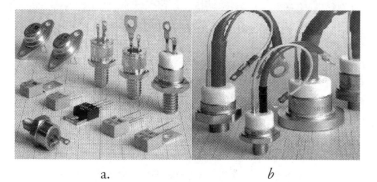

a.   b

Figure 6.1: a & b Thyristors and triacs (*courtesy of microElectronika*)

Thyristor is an enhanced diode. Besides anode (A) and cathode (k) it has another lead which is normally described as a gate (G), as establish on picture 6.2a. The same way a diode does, a thyristor conducts current when the anode is positive compared to the cathode. Sufficient current is flowing into the gate to turn on the device only if the voltage on the gate is positive. When a thyristor starts conducting current into the gate, this is of no importance and thyristor can only be switched off by removing the current between anode and cathode. For example, see figure 6.2d. If S1 is closed, the thyristor will not conduct, and the globe will not light. If S2 is closed for a very short time, the globe will light. So S1 must be open to turn off the globe. Thyristors are marked in some circuits as SCR, which is a short form for Silicon Controlled Rectifier.

A triac is very similar to a thyristor, with the difference that it can conduct in both directions. It has three electrodes, called anode 1 (A1), anode 2 (A2), and gate (G). It is used for regulation of alternating current circuits. Devices such as hand drills or globes can be controlled with a triac.

Thyristors and triacs are marked alphanumerically, KT430, for example. Low power thyristors and triacs are packed in same housings as transistors, but high power devices have a completely different housing. These are shown in figure 6.1. Pin-outs of some common thyristors and triacs are shown in 6.2 a and b. Diacs (6.2c), or two-way diodes as they are often referred to, are used together with thyristors and triacs. Their main property is that their resistance is very large until voltage on their ends exceeds some predefined value. When the voltage is under this value, a diac responds as a large value resistor, and when voltage rises it acts as a low value resistor.

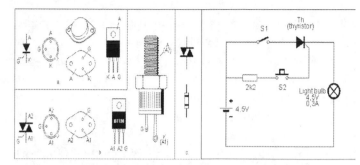

Figure: 6.2: Symbols and pin placements for: a - thyristor,
b - triac, c – diac, and d - principle of operation of a thyristor
(*courtesy of microElectronika*)

6.1 Thyristor Practical circuits

When light is present in a room the circuit of figure 6.3a
detects it. With no light, the photo-transistor does not
conduct. When light is present, the photo-transistor
conducts and the bell is activated so alarm starts. The
alarm is turned off via S1 because turning off the light will
not stop it.

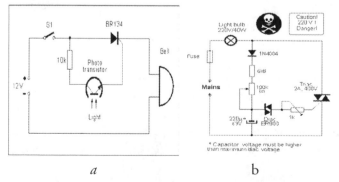

a   b

Figure 6.3: a-Alarm circuit using a thyristor and a
photo-transistor b-Flasher (*courtesy of microElectronika*)

Figure 6.3b above shows a circuit used to flash a globe. This circuit flashes a 40w globe several times per second. Mains voltage is regulated using the *1N4004* diode. The 220uF capacitor charges and its voltage rises. When this voltage reaches the rating-voltage of the diac (20v) the capacitor discharges through the diac and into the triac. This switches the triac on and lights the bulb for a very short period of time, after sometime (set by the 100k pot), the capacitor is charged again, and the whole cycle repeats. The 1k trim pot sets the current level which is needed to trigger the triac in the setup.

Another control circuit design to run the brightness of a globe or the speed of a motor is shown in figure 6.4 below.

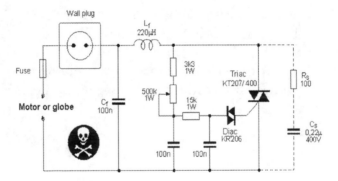

Figure: 6.4: Light bulb intensity or motor speed controller circuit
(*courtesy of microElectronika*)

Since the main use for this circuit is to control the brightness of a light bulb, then RS and CS are not needed.

Chapter Seven
Integrated circuits(IC)

The IC (Integrated Circuits) plays an imperative part in electronics. A lot of them are specifically made for an explicit task and contain up to thousands of transistors, diodes and resistors. Special purposes IC's such as audio-amplifiers, FM radios, logic blocks, regulators and even whole micro computers in the form of a micro controller containing several millionths of transistors can be fitted inside a tiny package. Some of the simple Integrated Circuits are depicted in figure 7.1below.

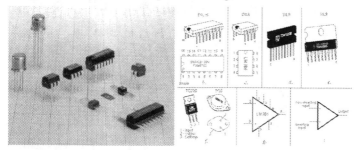

Figure: 7.1: some common Integrated circuits their symbols and pin-outs (*courtesy of microElectronika*)

Integrated circuits can be divided into two groups depending on the way they are manufactured, these are hybrid and monolithic. Hybrid circuits have been around longer. If a transistor is opened, the crystal inside is very small. This means a transistor doesn't take up very much space and many of them can be fitted into a single Integrated Circuit to form a single component.

The terminology used for most integrated circuits construction having two rows of pins is Dual In Line, DIL package. (DIL16 and DIL8 are shown in 7.1b and 7.1c). The pins are numbered in an anti-clockwise direction while viewing the device from the top and high power integrated circuits can generate a lot of heat as they have a metal tag that can be connected to a heat-sink for excessive heat dissipation. These IC's are shown in 7.1d and 7.1e, and 7.1f. Some symbols used to standing for integrated circuits are shown in 7.1g and 7.1i, while for amplifiers the symbol in 7.1g is commonly used.

Another similar device in this family called operational amplifier is depicted in figure 7.1i. The signs + and - represent inverting and non-inverting inputs. For the circuit to operate the signal to be amplified is applied between one of the inputs and ground and supply.

Further division of integrated circuits can be into two groups namely **analog (linear) and digital**. An output voltage produced by linear circuits is continuous, that follows changes in the input. Typical of a Linear IC is represented by audio amplifier. If a signal from a microphone is connected to the input the output will vary in the same way as the voltage from the microphone. When this is observed on an oscilloscope, the signal on the output will be the same shape as the microphone's signal depending on the amplification of the integrated circuit the voltage will be higher. The digital IC's are different because their output voltage is either LOW or HIGH not continuous that quickly changes from one state to the other.

7.1 Integrated circuits (Analog type)

In this topic, we will study LM386 IC that has all the components for a complete audio-amplifier as shown in figure 7.2. This figure illustrated example of an amplifier made with this integrated circuit, which can be used as a full amplifier for a walkman, interphone, cassette player or some other audio device. It can also be utilized as a test circuit for troubleshooting in electronics.

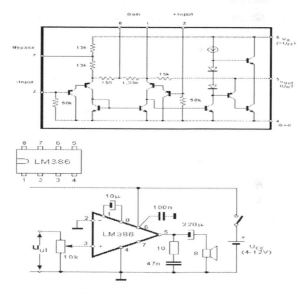

Figure: 7.2: LM386 arranged as low frequency amplifier
(*courtesy of microElectronika*)

The non-inverting input (between pin 3 and ground) is where the signal is connected while the Inverting input (pin 2) is coupled to ground. If 10µF is positioned between pins 1 and 8 a voltage amplification of 200 is formed. If this capacitor is detached the amplification is

20. It is possible to get in-between amplification by adding a resistor and linking it in series with the capacitor.

The 100nF capacitor which is placed between pin 6 (and joined to the positive of the supply) and ground is also important in this circuit. It should be ceramic and mounted as close to the integrated circuit as possible. It is a common practice when running with integrated circuits, not necessarily shown in the diagram when a capacitor is attached between the positive and negative, it stabilizes the voltage and protects the circuit from spikes. This is due to inductance in the power supply allowing high currents taken by the IC to upset its operation in the setup.

7.2 Integrated circuits (Digital type)

In this case a 14 pin DIL package IC CD4011 will be used to illustrate the main characteristics of digital circuits. This has pin-out shown in figure 7.3a. The small half-round slit on one end of the IC identifies pin 1. Pins 7 connected to negative and 14 connected to positive of a supply (battery or DC power supply).

Four logic NAND gates in a CD4011 IC each having two inputs and one output is employed. For gate N1 the inputs are pins 1 and 2, and output is pin 3. The symbol for a NAND gate is displayed in figure 7.3b. The inputs are marked A and B and output is F. Voltage for its supply can be up to 16v and as low as 5V. The output will bring up to 10mA at 12V but this is condensed as the supply voltage is reduced. Figure 7.3b shows the truth table for a NAND gate. It shows the output voltage (voltage between

F and ground) with different input states. There are only two voltages for every pin and are called states, with logic zero when the voltage is zero, and logic one when the voltage on the pin is the same as the supply voltage.

With this the second row of the truth table can be read: if logic zero is on both input pins, output is logic one, third row is similar: if the first input is one, and the second one is zero, output is logic one, fourth row: if the first input is zero, and the second one is one, output is logic one. For fifth row is different, since both of its inputs are one, here the definition of NAND gate states that the output is zero level.

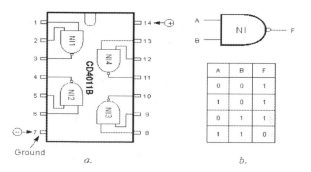

Figure: 7.3: a) - CD4011 pin placements, b) - symbol and the truth table for NAND gates (*courtesy of microElectronika*)

Logic circuits have many applications, but their main use is in computer circuits. The following circuit is a simple example to show how the gates can be connected to produce a project that turns on a globe when a finger is placed on a "touch pad." The globe turns off after a period of time, determined by the value of the 470u and 2M2 resistor.

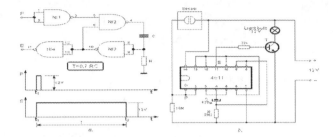

Figure: 7.4: a) The operation of a NAND gate,
b) Sensor switch using IC CD4011(*courtesy of microElectronika*)

By considering the circuit of figure 7.4a above, one realizes that both inputs of NI1 are connected to each other, so when input P is HIGH, the output is zero. This logic zero is passed on to NI2, so no matter what is on the input 6, output 4 is logic one. This means that between the ground and pin 4, the voltage is equal to 12V.

The capacitor C begins to charge as current flows through it and resistor R. Note that all uncharged capacitor behaves like a short circuit. So when 12V appears on pin 4, it is also present on resistor R and also on pins 8 and 9. Pin 10 shows logic zero for the reason of this which is connected to pin 6. From now on, logic zero on pin 5 is no longer needed because only one input needs to be zero for the output to be logic one. Therefore input P is no longer needed. Gates NI2 and NI3 maintain logic zero on pin 4. This will last depending on the value of the capacitor and resistor. As the capacitor charges, the voltage on the resistor drops and when it falls to 1/2 of the supply voltage (6V in our case), NI3 detects a low on its inputs so logic one appears on pin 10. Since logic one is now on input 5 (no logic one present on P), and on input 6, output 4 is zero, capacitor dumps its charge via diodes on the inputs on pins 8 and 9 and the circuit starts operating once more.

For a certain period of time equal to T=0.7RC the output of pin 10 at logic zero.

During that time output E (pin 11) is logic one. For example, if R = 2M2 and C=47µF, for time T = 2.2X10^6X47X10^-6 = 94 sec from the moment impulse on input P subsided while voltage on output E is 12V. The result of this experiment is shown on diagram 7.4a. The short positive pulses appearing on P in the time t_1 caused a longer variable pulse on the output E. The circuit of 7.5b displays circuit which allows us to light a bulb using four NAND gates interconnected in the way shown on figure 7.5a. The sensor is two copper (or some other conducting material) plates glued to some non-conducting material (plastics, wood, etc.) in close proximity to each other. So, when the sensor is touched with the tip of a finger, the circuit will close. In this case 12V appears on input P, which in turn conducts the voltage to the output E, resistor R = 22k conducts base current and the bulb lights on. When the finger is removed, output E will last for 94 seconds, after which it goes to logic zero and the light goes out this time.

The maximum allowed collector current of transistor T as it is selected is higher than the current of the bulb.

The value current flowing through the bulb is found by dividing its power by its voltage. For instance, if its power P = 6W and voltage U = 12V, current through the globe I = P/U = 6W/12V = 0.5A or higher. Take note of the bulb starting or "turn-on" current which is about six times the operating current and the transistor must be able to pass this current for the bulb to light up.

7.3 Some practical examples

A stereo audio-amp circuit using a TDA4935 IC is shown in figure 7.5. The integrated circuit contains two separate pre-amps and stereo output with Left and right input signals marked UL and UD, which are brought to two inputs of the amplifier. The chip can be used in stereo mode of 2x15W amplifiers and the maximum output for each amplifier is 15W. This type of IC has built-in heat sink and overload protection.

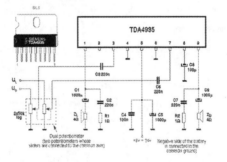

Figure: 7.5: Stereo audio-amplifier using the TDA4935
(*courtesy of microElectronika*)

In the second example, an audio amplifier using IC LM386 circuit with a preamp using a BC107 transistor is elaborated. The series capacitor coupled and resistor between pins 1 and 5 produces low frequency amplification (around 100Hz) improving the distinctiveness of the circuit. This type of amplifier could be used with any low frequency source like gramophone, microphone and so on.

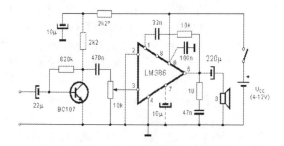

Figure: 7.6: complete audio-amplifier using the LM386
(courtesy of microElectronika)

Example number three is a simple alarm shown in figure 7.7 below. The circuit utilizes a CD4011 IC. The Gates NI3 and NI4 form a 600Hz audio oscillator. This signal is amplified using an NPN transistor and passed to an 8R speaker. To hear the 600Hz tone, connection to pin 8 is removed and connected to pin 9. This produces a constant tone. The Gates NI1 and NI2 form a 4Hz oscillator, whose output is connected to pin 8. This turns the 600Hz tone on and off at 4Hz. If pin 1 is connected to 7 via a switch this alarm can be used for home burglar purposes.

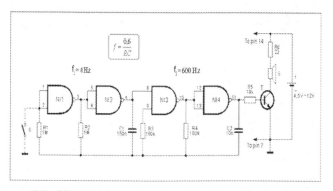

Figure: 7.7: CD4011 IC used as alarm *(courtesy of microElectronika)*

This chapter ends up with the last example of a circuit of mono FM receiver using a TDA7088T IC, along with the SMD components housed in a match-box along with two miniature watch batteries. Now, one can buy a ready-built scanning radio in a "junk shop" for as little as $US5.00 with stereo head-phones and analyze it.

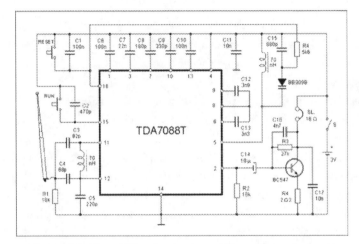

Figure 7.8: Mono FM radio receiver with an electronic preset
(*courtesy of microElectronika*)

The RUN button is used for tuning to a low frequency station automatically by pressing it. This turns on the part of the integrated circuit which is designated for scanning over a given range. The moment it finds a station it locks on until the RUN button is pressed again. When it reaches 108MHz it waits for the RESET signal which returns the scan to 88MHz. This can be done continuously when searching for other stations within the range.

Chapter Eight
Dynamic Speakers, Microphones and headphones

Speakers microphones, and headphones are components usually used as the input and output devices of many circuits. A microphone converts sound waves into electrical signals that closely follow the waveform of the sound being received. This signal is then amplified by the circuit and changed into a sound by a speaker or headphone. The symbols for these components are shown on 8.1below.

8.1. Symbols: a - microphone, b - speaker, c, d - headphones

Figure 8.1: Symbols of Microphones Speaker and headphones
(*courtesy of microElectronika*)

8.1 Speakers

A "speaker", or in the early days of radio "loud-speaker") is an electro acoustic transducer that produces sound in reaction to an electrical audio signal input. In other words, speakers translate electrical signals into audible signals. Today, the most conventional speakers use is the dynamic speaker. The dynamic speaker operates on the same basic principle as a dynamic microphone. When an alternating current (i.e., electrical audio signal input) is applied through the voice coil that is surrounded by a permanent magnet, the coil is forced back and forth as described by Faraday's law of induction, which causes the paper cone attached to the coil to respond with a rapid backward and forward movement that creates sound waves.

Normally, if high fidelity reproduction of sound is needed, multiple loudspeakers may be used, each reproducing a part of the audible frequency ranges. Small or miniature loudspeakers are found in devices such as radio and TV receivers, and many forms of music players. Larger loudspeaker systems are used for public address systems, music in theatres and concerts.

Typically housing for common speakers is an enclosure which is often a rectangular or square box made of wood or sometimes plastic. Another feature of a speaker includes its size and shape. It can be designed as crystal or capacitive.

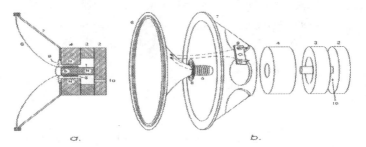

Figure: 8.2: Speakers (*courtesy of microElectronika*)

Ferrite rings (2, 3 and 4) shown in figure 8.2 in the cross-section of an electro-dynamic speaker are added to a large permanent magnet (1) which creates a physically powerful magnetic field in the narrow gap between magnets north and south poles. A Cylindrical former is added to the gap and it holds coil (5). The ends of the coil are taken to the outside of the speaker.

Resistance of a speaker is the value determined at a frequency of 1-kHz and is higher than its actual resistance and its wattage. Couples with its IMPEDANCE make two most important characteristics of a speaker. Familiar impedances are 4, 8 and 16 ohm, but there are also 1.5, 40 and 80 ohm speakers. Speaker wattages range from a fraction of a watt to hundreds of watts practically.

Largest speakers are more efficient and produce the least distortion especially in the low frequency range. So, choosing a speaker it is advisable to choose large ones. To get overall quality of the sound, speakers should be housed in a large box since it functions as a resonating compartment.

8.2 Microphones

Among the many types of microphone is the carbon, dynamic, crystal and capacitive. Carbon microphones mainly used in telephone applications were one of the first to be invented. Unfortunately, they are very noisy as the carbon granules rattle when the microphone is moved but later advanced types replaced them.

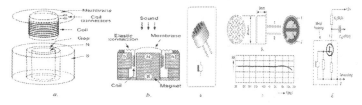

Figure: 8.3: Microphone (*courtesy of microElectronika*)

Basically, apart from the size dynamic microphone are exactly the same as a speaker, although they have a limitation of very low output but their quality of reproduction is marvelous. They are used in the recording industry for music and speech where high fidelity is required. The internal arrangement is shown in figure 8.3. A fine copper wire is wounded on paper cylinder and connected to a membrane which moves under the force of sound pressure created by the sound source. This coil is in a narrow gap with a high magnetic field produced by a permanent magnet. When the coil moves in this magnetic field, it produces a voltage the same to the sound causing the movement.

Dynamic microphone has a low resistance (impedance) and it usually needs a transformer as to be connected to an amplifier (called a pre-amp). This transformer is habitually built into the microphone's case, but if is missing, connecting the microphone to a preamplifier with low input resistance is compulsory.

For the type of microphones containing a crystal called a "piezo crystal" that is connected to a small diaphragm hence the name crystal microphone. When sound waves strike the diaphragm, the crystal changes shape and it produces a voltage that is passed to an amplifier. Just of recent, capacitive microphones have enhanced in quality and taken over from nearly all other types of microphone. They are small, rugged, and low in price while they produce a very high quality output. The shape, size and characteristics are also shown in 8.3.

The microphone needs a DC voltage for its operation contains, therefore a Field Effect Transistor is incorporated in it. Figure 8.3d shows how a capacitive microphone is connected to a circuit. It needs a "load resistor" to limit the current to the FET and the output is taken across this resistor.

8.3 Headphones

Some of the many types of headphone are crystal and electromagnetic. The electromagnetic type is the most frequently used. They function in the same way as speakers, with obvious differences in construction, since they are planned for much lower power. Their main characteristic is their resistance (impedance), from a small number of ohms to a few thousand ohms.

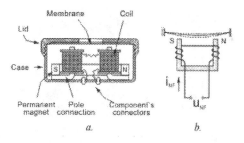

Figure: 8.4: Headphone (*courtesy of microElectronika*)

An electromagnetic headphone cross sectional view is shown in figure 8.4. It consists of a horseshoe magnet with poles that hold two coils. These are joined in series. The diaphragm is a thin steel plate so that when current flows through the coils, the diaphragm is pulled towards the coils. This moves the air and the results in a realistic reproduction.

8.4 Practical examples

A schematic diagram of a very simple FM radio-transmitter is shown in figure 8.5 below. It uses a capacitive microphone to transmit on a frequency between 88MHz and 108MHz.

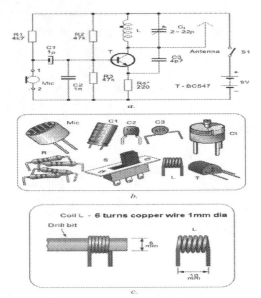

Figure: 8.5: FM radio transmitter circuit

(courtesy of microElectronika)

Let's consider the FM transmitter circuit diagram shown in figure 8.5 above. The transistor, coil L, trimmer capacitor C_t, capacitor C_3 and resistors R_2, R_3 and R_4

formed an oscillator with a frequency determined by the equation:

$$f_o = \sqrt[2\pi]{L(C_1 + C_{CB})}$$

eqn…10

C_{CB} represents the capacitance between the collector and the base. The value of this capacitance depends on the voltage in the base of the transistor.

The lower the voltage the higher the capacitance and the reverse is the case. When there is no sound, the voltage on the base is constant which means the frequency of the oscillator is constant. As the microphone picks up a sound, this will directly be passed to the base of the transistor via C_1 causing the frequency of the oscillator to change and that's why the circuit is called FREQUENCY MODULATED (FM) circuit.

When it is desired to transmit on a frequency away from any other radio station, a trimmer capacitor is incorporated. This transmitter has a range up to 200 metres, depending on the length of the antenna and where it is positioned. Preferably, the antenna should be vertical and as high as achievable. Ideally, the antenna can be as long as 3 metres but 180cm will work very well.

The coil labeled L is made by winding 6 turns of 1mm enameled wire using a 6mm diameter drill bit. This coil can be prolonged or compacted to adjust the operating frequency of the circuit and the trimmer will fine tune the frequency needed.

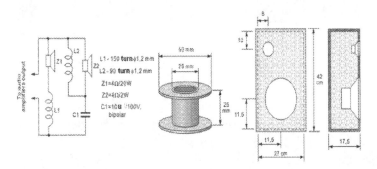

Figure: 8.6: Speaker circuit and casing (*courtesy of microElectronika*)

The main reason for using good-quality speaker is to be able to reproduce High Fidelity (Hi –Fi) sound. These are used in radios, TV's, cassette players, CD players, and the rest. Normal housing of a speaker is speaker boxes to accommodate at least two or more speakers since no individual speaker is capable of reproducing the full range of frequencies. Any speaker with a large cone is called a "woofer" and will imitate the low frequencies. A speaker with a small cone is called a "tweeter" and will replicate the high frequencies. Together, they will reproduce the full range of between 30-Hz and 15-kHz frequencies.

To detect the low or high frequency and redirect the correct frequency to the particular speaker becomes a difficulty. This is the work of a cross –over network. Referring to figure 8.6 an inductor L_1 passes the low frequencies to speaker Z_1. A capacitor C_1 passes the high frequencies to speaker of impedance Z_2. Impedance Z_1 reproduces frequencies from 30Hz to 800Hz and Z_2 reproduces sounds with frequencies from 800Hz to 15-kHz.

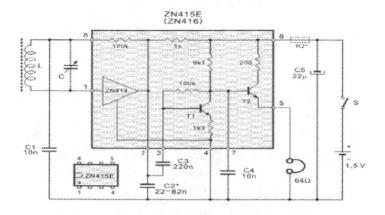

Figure: 8.7: Min AM radio receiver using IC ZN415E
(*courtesy of microElectronika*)

Most commonly portable devices such as radio receivers, cassette players, CD walkman, mp3 players, etc use headphones because they produce a very high quality reproduction of sound. All modern devices that have audio-amplifier built in integrated circuit are usually designed for 32 ohm headphones. Normal 8-ohm and 16-ohm headphones are also available in the market.

Figure 8.7 above shows schematic circuit diagram of AM portable radio built around the ZN416 integrated circuit. The output of this IC is connected to two serially connected 32-ohm headphones, which means 64 ohms is the overall resistance. There is a possible to join the radio receiver in figure 8.7 to amplifier in figure 7.5 by using a speaker output to produce a radio reception.

Chapter Nine
Components Opto-electronics

9.1 Photo diodes

Photo-electronic components also known as optoelectronic components are electronic components which generate light or react to it. A few components among them are Light Emitting Diodes (LEDs) photo transistors, photo diodes, photo resistors or 'LDR – Light Dependant Resistors', different visual indicators, light emitters and detectors, opto-couplers, and so on. Many of these components are familiar because of the "window" on the component's case which is used to pass the light through. Occasionally, a small lens, which directs light to some predetermined location inside the component, is put as an alternative of window. Figure 9.1 below depicts some of the most important optoelectronic components.

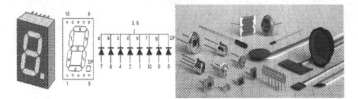

Figure 9.1: Photo-electronic components
(*courtesy of microElectronika*)

If a condition of the device either 'on or off' is needed, LED is the usual component put to do the job in circuits. LEDs normally come in various colors, shapes and sizes including, but most common ones are red, green and yellow. For the reason of more complication and manufacturing process, blue color cost a bit more than other color LEDs. They all have the same principles of use. Also they are identified as having square sizes, housed, SMD, angled, ultra bright, multicolored and many other kinds.

One frequent application of LEDs is the 'LED display' sequence. Figure 9.2 shows a typical LED display built around 8 diodes marked with an a,b,c,d,e,f,g and DP as 'Decimal Point'. These devices come in two possible flavors – with a common cathode.

Normally, protection resistors are connected to all diodes similar when working with ordinary LEDs. The internal structure of photo diodes is similar to all ordinary diodes; only that photo diode has an exposed surface for light to fall onto. LED act as high value resistor while in dark because its resistance lowers as light gains in intensity. They are similar to photo resistors in their behavior and are polarized components.

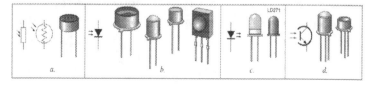

Figure 9.3: Opto-electronic components showing (a) resistors (b) Receiving light diodes (c) transmitting light diodes and (d) transistors (*courtesy of microElectronika*)

LED is one of the special kinds of photo-diodes. They include infra-red or ultra-violet emitting for different wireless communication purposes. Most widespread area of application of IR-LEDs (Infra Red) is remote controllers for TVs and other devices and circuits. The usual casing of photo diodes is metallic or square plastic cases with a glass window or a lens used to focus the incoming light.

Figure 9.3d the internal structure of a regular transistor has similar architecture with that of a photo-transistor. The only difference between them is the glass window which allows light to get to the crystal plate which holds all parts of the transistor.

When there is any change of light intensity, resistance between base and the collector varies, and this control variations of the collector current. Light has the same role as voltage over base of the regular transistor so, intensity rises, current through the transistor rises as well, and as intensity fades, current fades following the changes. Series of photo electronic components are manufactured in an array of different case shapes and sizes.

Another set of these components of interest in this topic are opto-couplers. They are extraordinary integrated circuits make possible out of an IR photo diode, and other component which is sensitive to light is photo thyristor. The emitter here is diode, and "receiving" end is the detector. Therefore, in this case a ray of light is only connection between the emitter and detector. The process is an important property of opto-couplers, because it allows two unusual parts of the circuit which operate on different supply voltages to connect to each other without actually conducting electricity. This means that one part could operate on 12V and other on 6V without fear of burning the sensitive lower voltage components in the circuit.

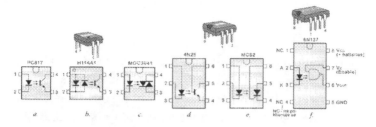

Figure 9.4: Opto-coupler Integrated circuits
(*courtesy of microElectronika*)

The structures of the Opto-coupler ICs in figure 9.4 above show how photo transistors are connected to other components in the same manner as ordinary transistors. The light that fall on it enable the control of current which passes through it. Control of is done by Voltage to the diode on figure 9.4a, this can be variable in time, but anode have to always be positive when compared to the cathode. In case this component is to function in an alternating current circuit, diode emits light only during one half of the interval in which anode is positive contrast to cathode. It is possible to use circuit on figure 9.4b in case it is desirable for diode to be lit during both periods. This circuit reveals two diodes in anti-parallel connection, so one of the two is lit during each half of the period.

Figure 9.4c is an opto-coupler using a thyristor. Thyristor is connected to other components in common manner, and it starts conducting only upon receiving light impulse initiated by the diode.

The transistor in figure 9.4d is controlled by regulating either the light intensity of the diode or voltage at pin 6, similar when using a triac circuit of figure 9.4e. Finally, the circuit is triggered by light intensity of the diode or voltage on pin6.

Figure 9.4f shows Dual input NAND gate circuit used as a detector. Normally, one of its inputs controls the voltage on pin 7, and the other is controlling the diode light intensity. Logic zero on pin 6 remains only in case pin 7 has a logic one and diode is lit up, pin 6 has logic one during all other cases.

9.2 Practical examples

Figure 9.5 shows a circuit diagram of device which detects a certain level of intensity of ambient light, and when that level is perceived, it turns on a device joined to mains grid. Data on figure 9.5 indicates that in absence of light resistance of the LDR resistor, NORP12, is R=1MegaOhm, which makes both base voltage and base current very low, so there is practically no current flowing through the transistor. Because there is no current flowing through the coil of the relay its other end is in switch-off position. When light intensity reaches certain point, resistance of the LDR lowers at arund10lx resistance, approximately 9kOhm. The makes voltages and current of the base to rise, this current then advances through the relay's coil which connects pins 1 and 3 and this switches on the desired appliance to the mains supply. Now, the slider of the 5kOhm trimmer resistor sets sensitivity of entire circuit. To lower the light level that triggers the appliance on, the slider's position is lowered. So, when trimmer is omitted from the circuit, greatest sensitivity is attained.

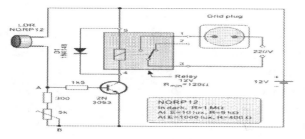

Figure 9.5: Detection of level of intensity of ambient light
(*courtesy of microElectronika*)

In the arrangement above, a photo-diode can replace the LDR. This is achieved when the cathode goes up, to + of the battery, or a collector of a photo-transistor goes up. This device will be off when light is absent in case regular resistor 47kOhm is placed in alternative, and LDR between points A and B.

Every relay in this circuit has a coil which agrees to 12V as voltage of the battery. The resistance of the coil is several hundreds of Ohms, and will not be lower than 120Ohm. The current through the relay should be equal to or greater than needed by the device plugged to the supply terminal. For instance, to find current draws by 5kW electric heater requires;

$$I = P/U \quad = 5000W/220V = 22.73 \text{ A.}$$

That is why any TUN transistor whose maximum current rating is higher than current through relay rating, is alright. This value is calculated by dividing battery voltage with relay coil resistance.

Consider the work of a remote control over some devices like the one used between the TV and its remote controller. Several designs of IR emitting and receiving photo diodes are used explicitly in low range transmitters and receivers. Practice use of photo diodes between the sound source (hi-fi, radio receiver, TV) and headphones that removes the need for long cables is shown in figure 9.6 below.

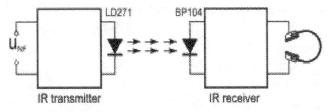

Figure 9.6: Radio transmission using IR light
(*courtesy of microElectronika*)

The low frequency signal uLF is to be carried and it is based on that frequency, IR transmitter modulates the high frequency voltage (carrier). This modulated HF voltage is further drove to emitting diode LD271. The changeable light emitted by this diode varies the resistance of the receiving diode, and thus the HF signal created using this variation is equal to the modulated signal on the transceivers end. While IR receiver is demodulating this signal, it is also transforming the received HF signal into the original LF signal which is equal to the original sound. Finally, this signal is further amplified and brought to headphones.

Another way of using optical components enables safe interface of different devices to a home PC. Figure 9.7 displays a simple way to interface a random device to the parallel printer port of the computer. Here, a small portable radio receiver that works using a 9V battery is connected. A male SUB-D 25 connector is used to connect the Receiver, battery and the interface to the parallel port. A program to control the circuit is developed using any programming language. A sample program written in Q-Basic is employed for this purpose. It will turn the receiver ON in 7am and turn it OFF in 7:30 am.

REM Wake up program 10 DO 20 LOOP UNTIL TIME$= "07:00:00" 30 OUT &H378, 128 40 SLEEP 900 50 OUT &H378, 0 60 STOP

The voltage on pin 9 will turn to +5V at exactly 7 o'clock and it will remain that way for the next 900seconds.

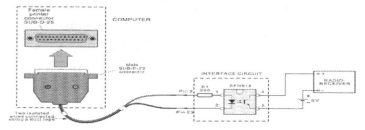

Figure 9.7: Control of radio receiver using a PC
(*courtesy of microElectronika*)

Finally, another diagram showing interface circuit is shown in figure 9.8. This enables connection of any device plugged to the mains grid to be turned on or off. Similar operation for control can be used over this device as done in previous program.

In accordance with the program pin 9 is +5V at logic one, diode will conduct electricity. The light emitted by it switches the triac inside the opto-coupler ON. This current flow through the 150-Ohm resistor and produce a voltage drop which ignite the triac, that enables current flow from the mains, and power the device. The maximum allowed current of the BT136 triac is 4A, showing that the maximum allowed power of the device is 990W. Notice that from what is learnt here, opto-couplers should be used only with resistance load devices ie, light bulbs, heaters...etc. It is recommended that using the relay interfaces is a good idea when connecting inductance load devices like electro motors and transformers.

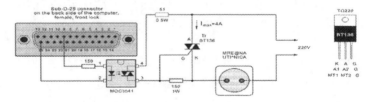

Figure 9.8: Interface using opto-coupler and triac

(*courtesy of microElectronika*)

References

[1] Filipovic D. Miomir (2006) Understanding Electronics components, microElectronika http://www.mikroe.com/en/books/keu/00.htm

[2] Horn, Delton T (1992) Electronic Components: a complete reference for project builders Tab Books publisher

[3] Horn, Delton T (1993) How to test almost everything electronic Tab Books, publisher

[4] Horn, Delton T (1989)Basic electronics theory--with projects and experiments Tab Books, publisher

[5] Dossis, Nick (2013)Basic electronics for tomorrow's inventors McGraw Hill publisher

[6] Motorola Semiconductor Data Manual, (1989) Motorola Semiconductor Products Inc., Phoenix, AZ,.

[7] Graf, Rudolf F and Sheets, William (1992) Encyclopedia of Electronic Circuits, Vol. 4 Granite Hill Publishers

[8] Dunton, John (2007), Practical Electronics Handbook Elsevier Science and Technology publisher.

[9] Brindley, Keith (2011) Starting electronics Elsevier Publishers

[10] Chattopadhyay, D(2006) Electronics Fundamentals and Applications) New Age International, publisher

About the Author

Born at Kazaure, **A. M. Yusufu** obtained his Higher National Diploma and Post Higher National Diploma in Electronics and Telecommunication Engineering at Kaduna Polytechnic, 1997. He has his Masters degree (M. Eng (Electrical) at Bayero University Kano 2003 and attended Communication Technology Courses in Sparta NJ USA in 2004. A full member of Nigerian Society of Engineers (NSE) and COREN registered. Currently, he is pursuing his PhD studies in Communication and Network Engineering in the University Putra Malaysia (UPM). His research interests include Photonics, Electronic & communication, Renewable Energy and Laboratory Work.

Yunusa Ali Sai'd was born in Uke. He received his Higher National Diploma in Electronics and Telecommunication in 1998 from Kaduna Polytechnic, and P(HND) in Electronics and telecommunication in 2000 from Kaduna Polytechnic, and M.Eng (Electrical) in 2004 from Bayero University Kano, Nigeria. A full member of Nigerian Society of Engineers (NSE), COREN registered and IEEE member, Currently he is pursuing the Ph.D. degree in Electronic Engineering at University Putra Malaysia (UPM). His research interests include Robotic mapping, Electronic Engineering, Laboratory Equipment and Renewable Energy.